Brands We Know

Transformers

By Sara Green

Bellwether Media • Minneapolis, MN

Jump into the cockpit and take flight with Pilot books. Your journey will take you on high-energy adventures as you learn about all that is wild, weird, fascinating, and fun!

This edition first published in 2017 by Bellwether Media, Inc.

Library of Congress Cataloging-in-Publication Data

Names: Green, Sara, 1964- author.
Title: Transformers / by Sara Green.
Description: Minneapolis, MN : Bellwether Media, Inc., 2017. | Series: Pilot:
    Brands We Know | Grades 3-8. | Includes bibliographical references and index.
Identifiers: LCCN 2016036846 (print) | LCCN 2016037066 (ebook) | ISBN
    9781626175563 (hardcover : alk. paper) | ISBN 9781681033037 (ebook)
Subjects: LCSH: Transformers (Fictitious characters)--Juvenile literature.|
    Transformers (Fictitious characters)--Collectibles--Juvenile literature.
Classification: LCC NK8595.2.C45 G74 2017 (print) | LCC NK8595.2.C45 (ebook)
    | DDC 688.7/2--dc23
LC record available at https://lccn.loc.gov/2016036846

Editor: Christina Leighton   Designer: Josh Brink

Printed in the United States of America, North Mankato, MN.

Table of Contents

What Is the Transformers Brand?

Megatron and the Decepticons attack a power plant to steal its energy. Will the city lose its electricity and leave people in the dark? Suddenly, a number of vehicles arrive and change into giant robots. It is Optimus Prime and the Autobots! The Transformers begin to battle. The Autobots are too strong for the Decepticons. Megatron and his followers flee. The humans are safe for now!

Transformers are toy robots that can change into vehicles, weapons, and other machines. The Transformers **brand** also includes comic books, video games, television shows, and movies. Fans use its **apps** to jump into action on mobile devices. Two toy companies own the Transformers brand together. One is called Hasbro, Inc. Its **headquarters** is in Pawtucket, Rhode Island. The other is called Takara Tomy. Its headquarters is in Tokyo, Japan. Millions of people around the world recognize the Autobot symbol. Transformers is among the most popular toy brands on Earth!

Optimus Prime

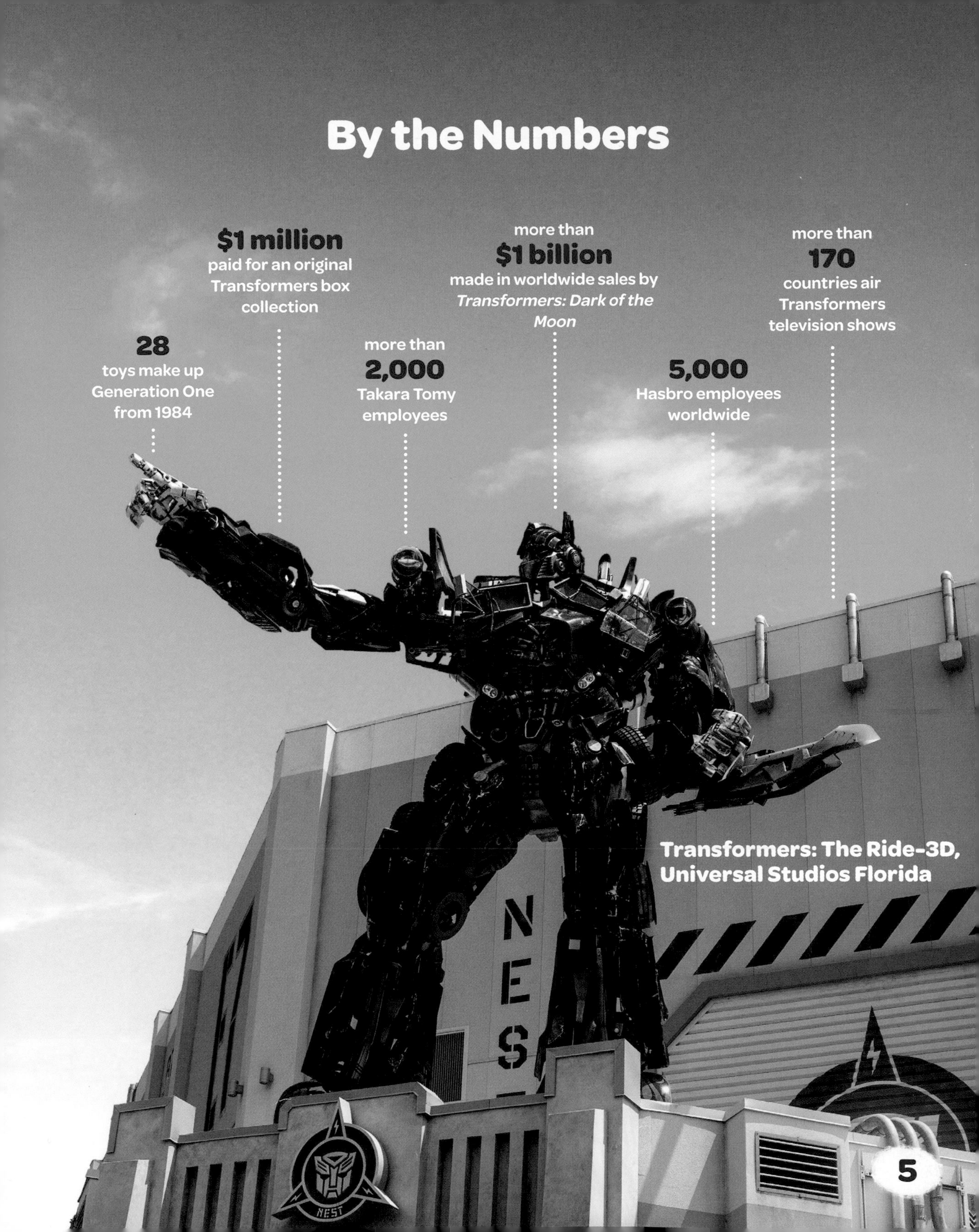

By the Numbers

28
toys make up
Generation One
from 1984

$1 million
paid for an original
Transformers box
collection

more than
2,000
Takara Tomy
employees

more than
$1 billion
made in worldwide sales by
*Transformers: Dark of the
Moon*

5,000
Hasbro employees
worldwide

more than
170
countries air
Transformers
television shows

**Transformers: The Ride-3D,
Universal Studios Florida**

Transforming Toys

The idea for Transformers came from other toy lines. In the 1970s, Takara made a Combat Joe action figure to follow the success of Hasbro's G. I. Joe. Low sales led the Japanese company to change the toys. They became Henshin **Cyborg** figures. These alien cyborgs had colorful parts and metal heads that could be switched out. The alien cyborgs then turned into the smaller Microman toy line. Microman figures also had **interchangeable** parts.

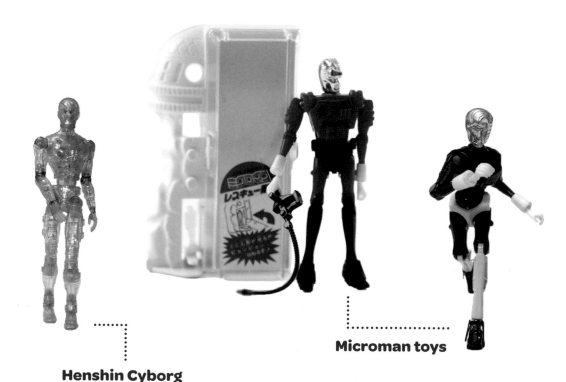

Henshin Cyborg

Microman toys

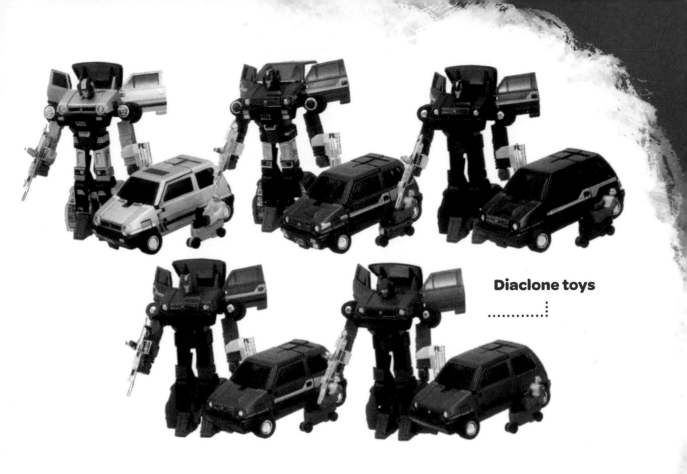

Diaclone toys
...........:

Takara then launched a toy line called Diaclone in 1980.
It featured robots that could disguise themselves as cars.
They were driven by Microman-like figures called Inch Men.
Popular car robots included Sunstreaker and Jazz.
Soon after, Micro Change toys were introduced. These
robots could change into guns, **cassettes**, and other
forms to disguise themselves and help Microman fight
enemies. Some of the Diaclone and Micro Change toys
eventually became Transformers!

Generation One

The 1983 Tokyo Toy Show led to an important partnership. A Hasbro employee attended the show and noticed the Diaclone and Micro Change toys. Hasbro staff thought the toys had great promise. The company bought the **rights** from Takara to sell the toys. It combined the two lines into one and named it Transformers.

Hasbro wanted to **market** the Transformers in creative ways. The toys needed names and personalities. They also needed an exciting story. Hasbro teamed up with Marvel Comics, known for creating Spider-Man and the Avengers. They created a story about alien robots called Transformers from the planet Cybertron. The robots could change their bodies into machines. The Transformers split into two battling groups. Optimus Prime led the good Autobots. Megatron led the evil Decepticons.

More than Meets the Eye!

1980s-current tagline

A Bee and a Bug
Bumblebee was originally a Volkswagen Bug. He is now a Chevrolet Camaro.

Generation One Transformers (1984)

Transformer	Alternate Mode	Job
Autobots		
Bluestreak	silver sports car	gunner
Bumblebee	mini yellow Volkswagen	spy
Jazz	white and blue sports car	special operations expert
Mirage	blue race car	spy
Optimus Prime	red, gray, and blue semitruck	commander
Ratchet	red and white ambulance	medic
Sideswipe	red sports car	warrior
Wheeljack	white, green, and red sports car	mechanical engineer
Decepticons		
Frenzy	blue cassette tape	warrior
Megatron	gray gun	commander
Ravage	black cassette tape	secret attacker
Rumble	red and blue cassette tape	demolition expert
Skywarp	black and purple jet	warrior
Soundwave	blue cassette recorder	communications officer
Starscream	red and gray jet	aerospace commander
Thundercracker	blue and red jet	warrior

Bluestreak

Mirage

Soundwave

Wheeljack

Optimus Prime

Ravage

Hasbro launched Transformers in the United States in 1984. The company introduced the toy brand with a comic book series and a cartoon. People got to know Optimus Prime and the Autobots. They also met Megatron and the Decepticons. These robots attracted a large audience. The comic books and cartoon were a huge success.

Robots in Disguise

1980s–current tagline

The Transformers cartoon

At the same time, Transformers toys hit shelves. Kids could own many of their favorite characters and create their own battles. Many Transformers turned into cars and trucks. Some turned into guns or other objects. Combiner Transformers were also popular. They could be attached together to make a larger robot. Small Transformers called Mini Vehicles were available, too. This first line of Transformers toys was an instant hit!

New Lines and Movies

Hasbro made changes to the Transformers line in the early 1990s. It painted **Generation** One characters from 1984 with different colors. The company also introduced toys that did not transform. Many people were upset by this decision. They lost interest in the Transformers brand, and sales declined. Hasbro needed something different.

Wild Disguises
Some Transformers had more than one Beast Wars disguise. Megatron became a T-Rex or an alligator!

Rattrap ···········

···········• **Megatron**

TRANSFORMERS™
BEAST WARS®

The company launched the Beast Wars toy line
in 1996. These Transformers looked like animals and
insects. They included a rat called Rattrap and a wasp
called Waspinator. The Autobots were now known as
Maximals, and the Decepticons were called Predacons.
During that time, the Beast Wars cartoon series also
debuted. It was a huge hit. People also enjoyed playing
Beast Wars video and card games. Beast Wars helped
save the brand. Transformers was popular again!

Movies helped Transformers become even more successful over time. The first **animated** Transformers film came out in 1986. It featured new and old characters. Hot Rod and other toys based on the movie became top sellers.

The first Transformers **live-action** movie was released in 2007. Autobots, Decepticons, and humans battle in the movie. They fight over the AllSpark that gives life to the robots. The movie gave the brand a huge boost. It made more than $700 million worldwide at the **box office**!

More Transformers movies followed. The 2011 and 2014 movies made more than $1 billion each at the box office worldwide. The movies led to the introduction of new toy lines such as MechTech and One-Step Changers. The next movie in the series is called *Transformers: The Last Knight*. More Transformers movies are planned after that. One is starring Bumblebee!

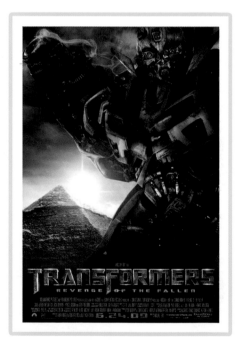

Their War. Our World.

2000s *Transformers* movie tagline

Beyond good. Beyond evil. Beyond your wildest imagination.

1980s *The Transformers: The Movie* tagline

Transformers Today

　　Today's Transformers are as exciting as ever. Popular toys include new versions of Chromedome, Mindwipe, and others from the Titans Return line. Victorion is part of the Combiner Wars series. She is made from six female Autobots. Helicopter robots form her legs. The Robots in Disguise Transformers feature Bumblebee and the Autobots. These toys can be scanned to unlock special features in a game. Many Transformers shows and comic books follow the stories of the new toy lines.

Harness the Power of Titan Masters

2010s Titans Return tagline

Gear up and roll out!

2010s Rescue Bots tagline

Rescue Bots

Transformers: Rescue Bots are designed for younger children. One robot becomes a bulldozer. Another turns into an ambulance. In the Rescue Bots cartoon, the robots work together to solve problems and protect a community. The series also focuses on teaching kids safety skills. These Transformers are ready to rescue people from danger!

....

Large Fortress

Fortress Maximus stands almost 24 inches (61 centimeters) tall. He turns into a battle station!

Transformers fans enjoy the brand in other ways, too. They gather at Transformers **conventions** each year. They can meet Hasbro team members and actors from Transformers movies and television shows. Toys, comics, and other items are also on display at these conventions. Fans can win prizes for the best Transformers costumes and artwork. Some conventions also have an **auction** for a **charity**.

Many fans play Transformers mobile games with friends. Popular games include Earth Wars and Robots in Disguise. Players select their favorite Transformers characters to fight.

A Transformers ride at Universal Studios is a fan favorite. This award-winning ride brings visitors straight into battle. The world of Transformers is full of adventure. Fans cannot wait to see what the Transformers brand turns into next!

Transformers ride at Universal Studios Singapore

Hall of Fame

Hasbro created a Transformers Hall of Fame in 2010. It honors important people and characters of the brand.

"Autobots, transform and roll out!"

– Optimus Prime

Transformers Fan Convention

19

Transformers Timeline

1972
Takara toy company develops the Henshin Cyborg action figure

1984
Hasbro launches the Transformers toys, comics, and cartoon

1980
Takara launches Diaclone toys

1986
The Transformers: The Movie is released in the United States

1974
Takara introduces Microman toys

1983
Hasbro discovers Diaclone and Micro Change toys at the Tokyo Toy Show

1993
Transformers: Generation 2 is launched

TRANSFORMERS BEAST WARS

1996
Beast Wars debuts

2010
Transformers Hall of
Fame opens

2011
The first-ever Transformers:
The Ride-3D opens
in Singapore

2002
Mini-Cons are introduced

2015
The cartoon
*Transformers: Robots
in Disguise* debuts

TRANSFORMERS

2005
The Transformers
Cybertron line debuts

2011
The cartoon series
*Transformers:
Rescue Bots* is
launched

2007
The live-action
movie *Transformers*
is released

Glossary

animated—produced by the creation of a series of drawings that are shown quickly, one after the other, to give the appearance of movement

apps—small, specialized programs downloaded onto smartphones and other mobile devices

auction—a public sale where goods are sold to whoever offers to pay the most money

box office—a measure of ticket sales sold by a film or other performance

brand—a category of products all made by the same company

cassettes—plastic holders containing reels of tape that play audio or video

charity—an organization that helps others in need

conventions—meetings for people who share a common interest

cyborg—a person with mechanical parts and physical abilities greater than an average human

debuted—was introduced for the first time

generation—a group from the same time period

headquarters—a company's main office

interchangeable—able to be changed out and used in place of one another

live-action—films that are not made by animation; live-action movies feature human actors.

market—to promote and sell a product

rights—the legal ability to use a certain name or product

To Learn More

AT THE LIBRARY

Bellamo, Mark. *The Ultimate Guide to Vintage Transformers Action Figures*. Iola, Wisc.: Krause Publications, 2016.

Furman, Simon. *Transformers: The Ultimate Guide*. New York, N.Y.: DK Publishing, 2004.

McCollum, Sean. *The Fascinating, Fantastic Unusual History of Robots*. Mankato, Minn.: Capstone Press, 2012.

ON THE WEB

Learning more about Transformers is as easy as 1, 2, 3.

1. Go to www.factsurfer.com.

2. Enter "Transformers" into the search box.

3. Click the "Surf" button and you will see a list of related web sites.

With factsurfer.com, finding more information is just a click away.

Index